Not Your Us
Christmas Jo

Let the Pun Begin…

By

Gary Rowley

Copyright © 2024 Gary Rowley

Not Your Usual... Christmas Joke Book

A frenzy of fun-filled, festive frivolity, generously packaged with 500+ side-splitting Christmas-themed jokes, puns and one liners.

Not a ho-ho-ho, snowman puddle, or bout of tinselitis in sight, this myriad of mayhem, mirth and merriment is the Christmas Joke Book everyone has been waiting for...a cringeworthy collection of perennial funnies, poking fun at everything we all love...*and hate*...about *the* most wonderful time of the year.

Forget the national elf service and Santa Jaws. Laugh your Christmas socks off at reams of real-life festive trials and tribulations instead, a fabulously funny original and classic jokes compilation, exploring the excesses, extremes and extravagances of a proper Crimbo; the shopping; the food and drink; hangovers and arguments; crap presents and rubbish telly; pubs, parties and fancy dress; a glut of New Year resolutions, diets and fitness drives.

Good, clean fun, *Not Your Usual* Christmas Joke Book is *the* must-have yuletide companion for festive fanatics everywhere. A perfect Xmas gift, dinner table accompaniment, or self-indulgent treat, it will leave you crying buckets of laughter, inadvertently basting the turkey and topping up the Buck's fizz as you unearth a constant stream of hilarious gems with which to torment family and friends and the not-so funny-funny man down the pub.

All you need to do to commence the punishment is sit back, relax, and slowly turn the page...

Let the Pun begin!

I ordered a book online called: How to Avoid Being Scammed At Christmas. A fortnight later, it's still not arrived…

All the missus could do was moan and groan when I asked if she wanted me to pick roast turkey and stuffing up on the way home. She said it was the worst mistake of her life, letting me name the twins.

Well, that's the big Christmas shop done and dusted. Just to be on the safe side, I chucked in a leaf blower, a bag of ready-mix concrete, two mouse traps and a kitchen sink…

I was on my way out of Asda with a stolen turkey, when this security man shouted, hoy, what do you think you're doing with that? I said, probably peas, sprouts, carrots, spuds and gravy, pal…

Just my luck. Two days before Crimbo and I've been diagnosed with Alice. I've no idea what it is, like…but apparently Christopher Robin went down with it.

I'm not saying we're poor…but I've just had Bob Geldof on the phone, offering to do a charity single for us.

A sign in the restaurant window said: Christmas Day dinners: taking bookings now. So I went inside and said, do you do takeaways? He said, of course, sir. I said, right…what's 989,845 minus 898,443?

The wife arrived home from Christmas shopping with a ladder in her tights. Credit where credit's due…she's one talented shoplifter.

A week after being made redundant, I got a job making advent calendars. It's true what they say…as one door closes, another one opens.

1st Turkey: I've got a job waitering this Christmas. 2nd Turkey: In your dreams, maybe. 1st Turkey: It's true. I've just heard the farmer say I'll be serving between ten and twelve.

The wife told me to put cranberry sauce on the shopping list. Now it's smeared red all over and she's going nuts because she can't read a word of it…

We ordered a new mattress for Crimbo, but the shop delivered a trampoline by mistake. The wife wasn't happy, I can tell you. Truth be known, she hit the flipping roof…

If anyone's wondering what's on telly this Christmas, just give me a shout…I've managed to get my hands on a 1979 copy of the Radio Times.

No doubt the flipping Titanic will be on again this year. Not to worry, though…it always goes down well.

I told the wife not to waste money buying me a new fishing rod for Crimbo. I said, I've just found one hidden behind the wardrobe.

I said, well, this time tomorrow, I'll be on the plane. She said, where are you going? Dubai? The Canaries? A fabulous festive cruise around the Caribbean? I said, actually, I'm shaving a couple of inches off the living room door.

A week before Crimbo, I started a new job as a perfume salesman and immediately had a pal of mine asking if I could get any festive freebies. I said, give me chance, mate…let me get my foot in the Dior first.

The kids want a puppy for Christmas. We were going to do a turkey, but hey…whatever keeps them happy.

Home-brewing a gallon of Crimbo cider wasn't the best idea I've ever had. I hurt my feet, crushing the woodpeckers…

The missus went spare when she found an empty whisky bottle under my pillow. I said, calm down…it was you who told me to get some Christmas spirit inside me.

Department store Father Christmas, swigging on a bottle of vodka on his way into a bauble and tinsel lined cave. Whey hey, I thought…Santa's blotto.

Richard Branson has put a bid in for our local footie team. Apparently his nephew wants a cowboy outfit for Christmas.

Newsflash: Animal rights protesters made off with 10,000 supermarket Christmas turkeys overnight. They have pledged to release them back into the wild once they have de-frosted.

Christmas shopping, I went in HMV. I said, do you have anything by The Doors? Assistant said, just what you see, pal…a pile of wire baskets and a fire extinguisher.

I'm not saying the cost-of-living crisis is hitting hard…but this year I'm going to wrap some batteries up for the kids with a note saying: Toys Not included.

What did pooch say to moggie when the tree went up? Now you're not the only one who's got an inside toilet…

I wrote to Santa, asking for a Porsche 911. He wrote straight back, telling me to at least be realistic. So I wrote, okay, I'll have a new girlfriend instead; someone who thinks I'm debonair, charming, handsome and witty, and will love and cherish me forever. He replied, and what colour Porsche would that be…?

I ordered a crystal ball two weeks ago. Only a few days now till Christmas and it's still not arrived. I might ring customer services and ask if someone can look into it…

I asked this shop assistant what aisle the pigs in blankets were on. He said, are your eyes bad, sir? I said, why do you ask? He said, because this is Sports Direct.

Trio of Irish lumberjacks, chopping festive spruces. Ooh look, I thought…tree fellers.

I went on the works Christmas do in a William Shakespeare costume. As soon as I walked in the pub, the landlord said, you…you're Bard!

A lorry spilled a yuletide delivery of smart TVs and laptop computers in the Toxteth area of Liverpool this afternoon. Police said the road was closed for nearly five minutes.

I just wanted to take this opportunity to wish everyone a very merry Xmas and a happy and prosperous new year. I've noticed people don't give much thought to yuletide messages these days. They just copy and paste some random crap then forward it on to all sundry. So, after all we've been through together this year, I just wanted to thank you personally for your friendship and wish you a fantastic 1968. All you need is love, best wishes John, Paul, George and Ringo. Love and kisses, Debbie, Alan & family xxx

June 29th and there's great news for insomniacs…only five more sleeps till Christmas.

I got a part-time job, delivering Amazon Christmas orders. First stop, there was a note on the door, saying: Dear Amazon man, please hide in blue bin. So I did. Now it's Boxing Day and I'm still here…

This psychic rubbed his crystal ball and told me to expect a white Christmas. I said, yeah, yeah, yeah…you can put the snowdome away now, pal.

I'm not saying the other half over did it with the Christmas shopping…but this 10p minimum charge for carrier bags: I've just calculated there's £1,688,291.90p in the cupboard under the sink.

The wife asked if she could have a locket for Crimbo. I said, if you've got a sore throat, darling, you can have a whole flipping packet.

I was going to buy my daughter the board game Operation for Christmas…until I found out there was an eighteen-month waiting list.

Er indoors keeps dropping big hints she wants a continental quilt for Crimbo. All she's been singing for days now is, duvet know it's Christmas…

I phoned 999 after my car was stolen with a boot full of freshly wrapped presents. Operator said, do you have a description of the driver? I said, no…but I think I got the number plate.

The missus asked what I'd got planned while she went Christmas shopping. I said, I'm not sure…I might go to Tenerife for a fortnight.

I went to the doctors with a mince pie growing on my head. He gave me some cream for it.

Some people need to get a life. It's not October yet and they're already letting fireworks off. One's just banged so loud, in fact, the cat ran straight up the Christmas tree…

Apparently the missus is buying me a stately home for Christmas. Anyone know where Sod Hall is…?

I was telling my mate how my new credit card arrived just in time for Christmas. He said, contactless, like? I said, don't talk daft, contactless. How would they have known where to send it…?

Did you hear about the bloke who nicked an advent calendar? He got 25 days…

I'm not saying it's rough in our neck of the woods…but I got a locally themed advent calendar and all the windows were boarded up.

Why waste money on an advent calendar? Just do what I do…walk round the kitchen, opening cupboard doors and eating anything in sight.

The office Christmas bash is a great opportunity to catch up with people you haven't seen…for at least twenty-five minutes.

I was doing the yuletide crossword. Sixteen across, I said: wish lists for Santa? She said, how many letters? I said, two, three billion at least.

Our kid's changed his name to Clinton and had Merry Xmas tattooed on his forehead. What a card…

I've landed a job waitering this Crimbo. The money's not brilliant, like...but at least I can put food on the table.

I turned up at the Christmas play with a book by Mary Shelley. The director screamed: I said Frankincense...not *Frankenstein*!

Thinking of treating the wife to a few days away over Crimbo, I phoned this hotel. Receptionist said, Best Western? I said, it's got to be either True Grit or The Magnificent Seven.

The wife self-identified as a Smurf, then left me Xmas Eve on account of my ongoing Elvis obsession. As she walked through the door, I began to sing, it's going to be a Blue, Blue Christmas without you...

I was in B&Q, looking for Christmas decorations, when a bloke in an orange apron came up and asked if I wanted decking. Luckily for me, I managed to get the first one in...

So, there I was, waiting for the missus, trying on Christmas dress after Christmas dress, when I suddenly got to thinking: how is it every time someone goes into the baby changing room they come out with the same child...?

I went to the bookshop. I said, do you have any books on Christmas turtles? Assistant said, hardback? I said, yeah, with little heads...

First day at the snowdome factory, I fell into a machine and found myself sealed inside a globe. Thankfully I'm alright, like...just a bit shaken.

I fancy going abroad for Crimbo. Trouble is, I hate flying. It doesn't half make my arms ache...

The girlfriend said it would mean the world to her if I put three Xs at the bottom of her Christmas card. Silly me...I don't think Karen, Sharon and Hayley was quite what she had in mind.

I was told to dress smart for my interview at the Christmas shop. So I turned up in a white coat, holding a test tube.

Thirty-seven weeks pregnant maybe, but it doesn't stop the woman next door disappearing on twice daily pre-Xmas shopping expeditions. Talk about shop till she drops…

I asked my mate how his new gun was going. He said, awesome; I shot a turkey with it today. Don't ask me why, like, but everyone in the supermarket ran a mile.

Short of cash for Crimbo, I was going to rob Peter to pay Paul…until I found out Peter had just paid his gas bill and he hadn't got anything, either.

My mate was telling me he went to see a Christmas Eve turn called The Arthritic Five. I said, don't tell me…it was a Stiff Little Fingers tribute act?

The wife wants me to buy her tickets to go and see The Buddy Holly Story in the West End over Crimbo. Yeah, right, I thought…that'll be the day.

I'd just finished my Christmas shopping when the mall was struck by a major power cut. Two flipping hours I was stuck on that escalator.

Don't believe these stories about me booking a holiday in the Indian Ocean over Crimbo. They're nothing but Mauritius rumours.

I've written a book about how to fall downstairs drunk properly at the office Christmas party. It's a step-by-step guide.

Letter to Santa: dear big fella: can I have a big fat bank account and a slim body? Please don't get things mixed up again like previous years.

Heading home for Crimbo, I jumped in this London black cab. I said, Waterloo, please. He said, you mean the railway station? I said, well, I'm a bit late for the battle, aren't I?

Good advice: avoid being sacked after having too much to drink at the works Christmas party by having too much to drink the night before.

I went to post my Christmas cards. On the way out of the post office, I was stopped by a security guard, who accused me of nicking a book of stamps. I didn't mess about, like…I stuck one on him.

Well, here I am, sitting on a sofa that cost £3,500…lovely and warm in front of a fireplace valued at £2,500…watching the latest blockbuster films on a 90" smart TV worth £4,000…surrounded by the best Xmas decorations anyone could ask for. I'm so happy, relaxed and content, not even a crowd of John Lewis staff, nagging me to leave, can spoil my day…

My three favourite things are eating my parents visiting for Christmas and not practising punctuation.

I'm buying the missus a horse for Christmas, eighteen hands high. I'll let you know how she gets on.

Two women, Christmas shopping. One says, I've got a pair of boxer shorts for him indoors. Other replies, nice one…sounds like an absolute bargain to me.

1st Centipede: what do you want for Crimbo this year? 2nd Centipede: whatever takes your fancy, but remember…my sock drawer is full.

I asked the boss if I could work from home. He said, give your head a wobble, son…you're a department store Father Christmas.

I asked my mate was his favourite yuletide song was. He said, Last Christmas? I said, not specifically…I was thinking more all-time really.

Everyone thinks I'm playing the part of Santa at the office Christmas party. Little do they know, but I've got the perfect get out Claus.

What a mess the country is in. Ah well…only three more emergency budgets till Christmas.

I'm off to see a band called Prevention over Christmas. Let's hope they're better than The Cure.

Same as last year, the politicians' nativity play has unfortunately been cancelled…after the organisers struggled to find anyone to play the parts of the three wise men.

A bloke at the works Christmas do emptied a bowl of grated cheese over me. I said, that was mature, wasn't it…?

I'm considering selling my John Lennon collection to fund Xmas. Imagine all the PayPal…

I bought the wife a John Lennon embroidery kit for Crimbo. Sew, this is Christmas…

While we're on the subject, I wonder why John Lennon's mother named him after Liverpool Airport?

Noticing the girlfriend salivating when we walked past a pork and stuffing sandwich stall at the Christmas market, I thought I'd treat her. Yup, I walked her past again.

It melts my heart when people put little kisses on my Christmas cards…forever reminding me of a crush I had on my maths teacher at school, who obviously had a crush on me back…forever leaving kisses next to all my answers.

Tree up, the missus started soaking the uppermost branches in washing up liquid. Apparently she was just following instructions…putting the Fairy on top.

Out Christmas shopping, I decided to buy a first aid kit. Yup, I thought I'd treat myself…

I had my torso waxed on a yuletide charity do, disposing of the evidence in the pub log burner. And everyone started singing: chest knots roasting on an open fire…

Does anyone know where I can get any proper ice cubes for Crimbo? Seriously, I don't want any more of that frozen crap…

So, there I was, waiting to board my Christmas cruise, when this flash sports car pulled up and the captain got out. I said, how do you afford a car like that? He said, oh, I work for Cunard. I said, ar, I work f'cunard as well but I can't afford a flipping Lamborghini…

The wife asked what I'd got her for Crimbo. I said, see that pink Ferrari across the road…? Well, I've got you a pair of slippers the same colour.

I've just seen one, two, three women in a row, all dressed as yuletide spruces. I can't believe some people think it's still socially acceptable to wear fir…

So I said, er indoors went nuts when I got sozzled at the Christmas party, then didn't get in till turned midnight. He said, sore head, like? I said, saw red? Put it this way: I was lucky she didn't clobber me one…

I'd say sleeping in the nude is generally a good thing. Except, perhaps, during a Christmas getaway flight to the Caribbean…

Driving home for Christmas, I got stuck in a right old snarl up and finished up calling the Cones Hotline. An hour later, I was still in a queue…

I was doing a bit of pre-Xmas window shopping with the missus. I said, that's the one I'd get. Next thing, Cyclops had me by the throat saying, you wanna piece of me…?

What did Santa say to his helpers just before they loaded his sleigh? Come on now, lads, let's get this sleigh loaded up…

I've just received a Christmas card with Do Not Bend printed on the envelope. Two hours I've been here now, trying to work out how to pick it up…

I got a temporary Christmas job, filling up at Tesco. First morning, I rang the gaffer. I said, I'm just arriving on the south coast now, boss. He said, do you realise it's five in the morning? And what are you doing on the south coast? I said, just what you said, boss…making sure I was in Brighton early.

Hughie had *way* too much to drink at the office party. Talk about Christmas blooming heave…

For anyone planning a festive buffet, I'd heartily recommend the book Party Food Galore by Phil Yabootz.

The missus was supposed to be buying me a suitcase for Crimbo. Now I'm hearing on the grapevine she's got me Carry On Cabin Luggage. Sounds like the worst Sid James and Barbara Windsor film ever.

I sent my daughter to school dressed as a deep fat fryer for a book themed pre-Xmas fancy dress fundraiser. I said, if anyone asks… tell them you've come as page ninety-eight of the Argos catalogue.

The wife said she fancied an animal skin coat for Crimbo…so I bought her a donkey jacket.

I'm dreaming of a white Christmas. That stated, if the white runs out I'll happily drink Red…

Scores of workers, playing leapfrog at the office party. Whey hey, I thought…it's Christmas jumper day!

Haggling with a salesman over an Xmas bike, I said, what's the lowest you'd go on it? He said, two miles per hour. Any slower and you'll fall off.

Xmas warning: don't forget to buy enough food for at least 36 days. Because the shops will be closed for at least 36 hours.

I've given up drinking till Christmas. Sorry, bad punctuation. Should read: I've given up, drinking till Christmas.

The doctor wasn't remotely interested when I showed him a big red boil on my backside. In actual fact, he completely ignored me…disappearing down the dairy aisle and carrying on with his Christmas shopping.

Don't believe all these scare stories about a Christmas gravy shortage. I've just come from the supermarket and they've plenty of *stock*…

Twenty squids to see Santa for one minute and all I got was a crap toy. What a rip off…I'm glad I didn't take the kids.

I bought turkey, stuffing, boiled and roast spuds, peas, carrots, sprouts, pigs in blankets, cranberry sauce and gravy in a can. It was my Christmas tinner.

I went to a Christmas Eve engine-themed fancy dress party in a piston costume. I didn't half look the part…

The missus asked for something silk for Crimbo, so I got her a tub of emulsion. No doubt it will be the wrong colour.

With the kids endlessly scouring the house, looking for Christmas presents, I took my mate's advice and put them in the attic. Big mistake…I didn't get a wink of sleep for listening them screaming as they crawled around amongst the cobwebs and spiders.

Tip: if you need frozen peas for Christmas dinner but are running short of cash…pretend to fall over in the supermarket and they'll give you a couple of packets free to hold over your make-believe injury.

Skint maybe…but it doesn't stop er indoors Christmas shopping like there's no tomorrow, going from shop to shop, flashing the plastic, saying, visa nice…visa'll fit…visa'll do.

A sign in the butchers said: Turkey £40. Not bad, I thought…that's a couple of grand cheaper than I was quoted at the travel agents.

I admitted I was contemplating throwing on the sick to spend Crimbo in Tenerife with the lads. The boss said, if it's true, I'm afraid I'm going to have to let you go. I said, wow, boss, cheers, boss…I always said you were the best gaffer ever.

Christmas Eve Down Under and Bruce accidentally rings Melbourne cricket ground when his wife is admitted to the birthing suite. Seeing the shocked look on his face, his mate asks what's wrong. Bruce replies, what's wrong? Sheila has gone into labour. They've got three out so far and the rest should be out by lunch. Oh, and one was a duck…

While the missus prepared for a yuletide Wham tribute act girl's night out in town, I headed off for a kip. I said, don't forget to wake me up before you go-go...

Tonight's movie premiere is Christmas Kissing Beneath Obligate Hemiparasitic Plants, starring Miss L Toe.

Christmas Day at 3pm, there's a special programme on all about His Royal Highness's favourite fruit. Yup, it's The King's Peach time...

When Roy Wood penned the lyrics, I wish it could be Christmas every day...I'll bet he hadn't spent half the morning driving round the local shopping centre, looking for a flipping car parking space...and then arrived home and realised he'd forgotten the sprouts and gravy mix.

Telling myself over and over that a dog is for life and not just for Christmas, I asked this bloke what his pit bull puppies were going for. He said, anything they can get their teeth into...

What does a kangaroo and a rhinoceros have in common? Neither will be unwrapping an Xbox Series X on Christmas morning.

My grandad always used to say that as one door opens another closes. Great bloke, like...terrible advent calendar maker.

It's sad how many Christmas traditions are dying out. I've just read an article saying that advent calendar days are numbered...

We were so poor growing up that I once opened an advent calendar door and there was a bailiff behind it.

It got so bad one year, in fact, I was given an empty Action Man box and told it was a deserter.

I had my credit card stolen over Crimbo but decided not to report it. Whoever nicked it was spending *way* less than the wife.

This newspaper headline read: Five Go To Court For Selling Counterfeit Christmas Goods. I thought, that sounds like the worst Enid Blyton book ever…

I told my mate I was writing a book on Christmas turkeys. He said, try doing it on paper, mate…you'll find it a lot easier.

The girlfriend says she wants Chanel no 5 for Christmas. Sounds simple enough, like. I'm just a bit worried about how difficult it will be to re-tune the Freeview box.

I arrived back at the car from Christmas shopping to find someone had stuck a plastic envelope on my windscreen, with a little note inside saying: Parking Fine. Aww bless, I thought…that's really nice of them to say so.

Christmas shopping, I went in PC World and enquired about Blu-ray. They put a call out and this bloke appeared. It said Raymond on his shirt and he was completely blue from head to foot.

I dipped into the Roses and found the tin was stuffed with pictures of Snoop Dogg, 50 Cents and Ice Cube. Alright, I said…who's put the rappers in the tub?

On a related topic, all I seem to have heard this Crimbo is Eminem songs. I think it must be the rapping-paper…ba-dum-tish!

I asked the gaffer if it was alright to finish a few days early for Crimbo. He said, don't talk wet…now get back in your grotto and get that red coat and false beard back on.

Can you believe it? Christmas Eve, still 10 weeks till pancake day, and shops are already selling flour and eggs…

I hate Christmas shopping. I've just queued an hour in Poundland only to be told they don't do quid gift vouchers.

Every festive season, my parents would bath me in cheap Australian lager. It wasn't until I was eighteen I realised I'd been Fostered.

Little known fact: on Christmas Eve 1604, Guy Fawkes set off on the long walk from York to London. It took him nearly a year to get there on account his shirt and trousers were stuffed with straw and scrunched up paper.

I've just seen a festive spectral presence on its way out of the driving test centre, smiling and wafting a piece of paper around. Ooh look, I thought…it's the ghost of Christmas passed.

That's it, Christmas is definitely ruined. I've just been told Chris Rea's car has failed its MOT.

24th December and first day as a London cabbie, I was asked to pick a passenger up from 221B Baker Street. Whey hey, I thought…driving Holmes for Christmas.

I went to the bar; I said; how much for lager? Barman said, six quid a pint or a tenner a pitcher. I said, just give me a pint…forget the photo.

Did you hear about the bloke who was arrested on suspicion of nicking a lorry load of Xmas trifles? He was remanded in custardy…

I made my fiancée's dreams come true by hiring a castle for our Christmas wedding. Not that you'd have known it…you should have seen the look on her face as we were bouncing around.

After getting more than a bit tipsy Christmas Eve, I stupidly promised the wife I'd make it up to her by taking her to Sydney to see the New Year celebrations. Now what do I do? If I let her down, there'll definitely be fireworks…

I decided to have a chat with the wife when the Wi-Fi went down over Crimbo. I couldn't believe it when she told me she didn't work at Woolworth's anymore…

Fact: it's not officially Christmas until you've told a roll of sellotape to ***k off!

Be vigilant if you're out drinking this Crimbo. I'm in the boozer now and I've just found a hedgehog in my pint. I thought, this has been spiked...

I went to a party in Michael Myers fancy dress. Yup, I was dressed to kill.

Blimey O'Reilly: I've just been hit by a tidal wave of festive tonic water. I was almost Schwepped away...

I told the wife I was packing it all in to go and work in pantomime. She said, oh, no, you're not! I said, oh, yes, I am!

I eventually auditioned for the part of a dwarf in Snow White, but didn't get it. I'm not Happy...

11.55pm on Christmas Eve, I'll be partaking in a spot of algebra, long division and by Pythagoras. Yup, I'm off to midnight maths.

The wife sent me out for six cans of Sprite for her Christmas Eve buffet...but I picked 7 Up by mistake.

I delivered pizza to a Dracula themed fancy dress party. A bloke in a cape with greased back hair and big fangs answered the door and said, don't just stand there. Come inside...we don't bite, you know.

As if last year wasn't bad enough, I've been invited for Christmas dinner again by the cannibal living next door. I've accepted, like...but if he offers me a leg again, I'll be making sure there's not a shoe and sock on it like last time.

Speaking of which, the same cannibal was kicked out of the army on account of his eating habits. Every time he had eggs for breakfast, he insisted upon having soldiers with them.

I was talked into going on a festive coach trip to see a band called The Pedometers. I wouldn't have bothered if I'd known it was a Steps tribute act.

Christmas Eve and the wife left me on account of my obsession with Blankety Blank. As if that wasn't bad enough, she took all the ------- with her.

I wonder if the residents of Emmerdale and Coronation Street buy Christmas TV mags to check what kind of Crimbo they're going to have...?

Bloke goes in a pub with a pair of jump leads round his neck. Landlord says, it is Christmas Eve, you know...you're not going to start anything, are you?

It's about time banks kept their flipping ATMs filled up properly. Three in a row I tried Christmas Eve and they all had insufficient funds.

I eventually found an ATM willing to dispense cash, but what a disaster that turned out to be. Free withdrawals it said. I checked later and guess what? They'd only gone and deducted it from my account...

Christmas week and we only get left two hundred houses and seventeen blocks of flats by the wife's long lost Uncle Arthur. As I was cracking open the champagne, she looked at me and said, I wouldn't get too excited if I was you...he was a flipping window cleaner.

Oh, go on, then...what do you call a reindeer with no eyes? Yup, no eye deer.

I visited my pal Christmas Eve and found the house stuffed floor to ceiling with tubular chairs. I said, where did this lot come from? He said, the doctor's waiting room. Every time I visit, the receptionist tells me to take a seat...

I went straight to A&E after falling down drunk. I said, no matter where I touch my body, it hurts. Doctor said, I'm not surprised...you've broken your finger.

Apparently Father Christmas has fainted on the luggage carousel at Manchester Airport. Paramedics are at the scene and have said not to worry…he's coming round slowly.

I nipped to the chemist Christmas Eve and there was this moggie, leaning on the counter, waiting for a prescription. Whey hey, I thought…puss in Boots.

Christmas Eve and I was watching a film with creepy organ music playing as a bloke entered a church. I shouted, don't go in, mate…it's a trap! The wife shouted, what's that you've got on, darling? I said, just our wedding video, dearest…

Two asses, Christmas shopping at the supermarket. *Lidl donkey, Lidl donkey…*

I poured half a bottle of Xmas gin on the front lawn. Ten minutes later, it was half cut…

The missus kept reminding me how she always struggled getting to sleep on Christmas Eve. I said, try kipping on the edge of the bed…you'll soon drop off.

Christmas Eve and I slept like a baby. First I crapped myself…then I woke up twice for a bottle of milk.

So I said to this policeman, you can't arrest me for giving someone a Christmas kiss. He said, you might call it a kiss, mate…but I think most people would refer to it as a headbutt.

I crept downstairs Christmas Eve and discovered the Devil, coming down the chimney with a sack of presents. Apparently my dyslexic son had written a letter to Satan…

It's been on the news that police arrested a man in stockings and suspenders on Christmas Eve afternoon. Bit odd…I'd have thought they would have at least kept their uniforms on.

Does anyone know the recipe for figgy pudding? Because I've had carol singers at the door for an hour now and it doesn't sound like they're going to leave until they've had some.

I had a pea shooter confiscated on my way into the Christmas carol service. The vicar said it was a weapon of mass disruption.

The girlfriend bought me a four-pack of Andrex for Crimbo. I don't think she quite got it when I said I was a big Lou Rawls fan…

Last Christmas, I got the kids a BMX each on the never-never. Big mistake. Huge, in fact. Now I'm caught up in a right cycle of debt.

Christmas week and I keep receiving anonymous deliveries of cashews, pistachios and almonds. Seriously, it's driving me nuts…

I was leaving work for the Christmas holidays when the gaffer shouted me back. He said, hang on a sec…I've got your cards for you. I said, but you know I don't do cards, boss. He said, well, you can do these…you're fired!

Bloke in a boozer, carrying five pints of beer, ten vodka and limes and sixteen packets of turkey crisps. I said, do you need a tray, mate? He said, do I heckers like…I've got enough to carry.

I went out Christmas Eve dressed as an iPhone, while my bezzie went as a sky rocket. After a brush with the law, I was charged and he was let off…

I wonder if Chris Rea made it home in time for Christmas? I'd be surprised if he didn't, like. I mean, he *did* set off in 1986, didn't he…?

The wife bought me a herd of cows and a milking barn for Crimbo. I knew I should have checked how to spell diary.

Just as bad, I bought *her* a can of lorry oil only to discover it's actually pronounced *L'Oréal*…

Christmas Day and the mother-in-law has been peering through the window ever since it started snowing. If it gets any worse, I'm worried I might have to have to let her in.

The wife and I have just watched Home Alone, It's a Wonderful Life, Jingle All the Way and Santa Claus the Movie back-to-back. Luckily, I was the one facing the telly.

I phoned my Nan; I said, what did you think to the African Grey talking parrot I got you for Christmas? She said, lovely, thanks…the meat just fell off the bone.

Er indoors got me a pair of baggy trousers and a trip on a night boat to Cairo for Crimbo. I thought, this is Madness…

I decided to cook an octopus for Christmas dinner…just in case everyone wanted a leg.

It's just been on the news that people will stop celebrating Christmas by 2050. I thought, what…by ten to nine tonight?

That new laptop I got for Christmas: I hit the Space Bar and finished up in a boozer on Saturn.

I love sprinkling traditional yuletide herbs on my turkey dinner. It's the most wonderful thyme of the year…

What a beautiful, crisp Christmas Day morning. It's only 9 o'clock and I've already had three packets.

Christmas 1974. Him: What's on the telly? Her: A table lamp, a few family photos, a pair of painted chalk ornaments from the fair and a pile of leftover change from this morning's visit to the Co-op.

To all the people who received a book off me this Christmas…please be reminded they are due back at the library Monday week.

With Christmas lights burning everywhere, I thought I'd do my bit for the planet. I unplugged a long line of electric cars that weren't going anywhere.

I'm not saying I'm puny, like…but I was given a Bullworker for Crimbo and couldn't get the box open.

The missus's big present from me this year was a thousand-page novel. She said, you know I love reading…but why a thousand pages? I said, it's a long story…

Every 25th December, I come over all sad and think of how many people I've lost down the years. I also wonder whether or not I should have chosen a different career than becoming a tour guide.

I'm not saying our neighbours are posh…but we were invited round for Christmas dinner and had pigs in duvets.

Three days it took er indoors to cook Christmas dinner. In her defence, she only did what it said on the back of the frozen peas packet…boil separately.

I ripped into a packet of crackers and thought to myself, nice biscuit…but where's the silly hat, cheap toy and corny joke?

Apparently, it's impossible to eat four crackers in a minute. Always up for a challenge, I downed three…but then nearly choked on a plastic moustache.

With excrement all over the lawn, roof tiles, chimney stack, hearth and living room carpet, I went to the foot of the stairs and shouted: he's been!

On the first day of Christmas, my true love said to me, blimey moses…this flipping oven's hot!

When the other half started leaving jewellery catalogues all over the house in the run up to Crimbo, I decided to take the hint. Yup, I bought her a magazine rack.

Wifey: I've got a couple of Christmas tips for you, dearest. Number one, forget the past, because you can never change it. Hubby: What's number two, darling? Wifey: Forget the present as well, because I didn't get you one.

It's always been a tradition in our house to go down the pub on Christmas Day, then return home and deck the halls. To be perfectly honest, I'm surprised the Halls have lived next door for as long as they have.

I've just entered the world's tightest Christmas bonnet competition. Hopefully, I'll pull it off…

Fifty years old and I get given a Meccano set for Crimbo. Seriously, I don't know what to make of it…

Asking for a friend: does a Christmas Day chocolate orange count as one of my five per day…?

I asked the missus for a Christmas present that goes from 0 to 100 in two seconds. She got me a set of bathroom scales.

I've just had Christmas dinner with a chess grandmaster. Never again, I can tell you. It took him two hours to pass the pepper.

Did you hear about the cannibal who wrapped up dismembered feet and armpits as stocking fillers for the missus. He thought she might like a few smellies.

Fisherman rips into his Christmas present from the wife. He says, a box of cornflakes? I said *sea reel*…not cereal!

Christmas morning and er indoors was in a right old mood, complaining she had piles and piles of ironing. I said, goodness, darling…I can't imagine which is worse.

Note to self: clear up Pringles, trodden into living room carpet. It's beginning to look a lot like crisp-mush…

I bought the wife a second-hand clock for Crimbo. She said, is that it? This had better be a wind-up…

The missus asked if I fancied going to see Cats in London over Crimbo. I said, nah…if it'd been a musical or something, I might have thought about it.

I bought the girlfriend a ladder for Christmas. She went up the flipping wall…

The missus thinks I don't know how to wire a plug on the hairdryer she got for Christmas. Well, she's in for a shock…

With Christmas dinner finished, the missus asked if I could clear the table. I needed a run up, like…but I managed it alright.

We're having a goose for Christmas dinner this year. Well, it's actually a turkey that thinks it's a goose…it's trans gander.

I wrapped some pieces of ripped-up cardboard and gave it to the lad for Crimbo. I said, there you go: that's what you asked for, isn't it? An ex-box…?

Warning: if anyone else receives a Dyson ball cleaner for Crimbo, please be warned…it's *not* for what it suggests on the box.

I got the wife a DIY colonic irrigation kit for Crimbo. She told me to stick it where the sun doesn't shine.

Well, that's Christmas Day night sorted. Gladiator 2 and a bottle of Scotch whisky. That's my kind of Slay-Bells…

I was tucking into my Christmas dinner when the phone rang. I said, I'll have to call you back…I've a lot on my plate at the moment.

Workmate rings, bragging he'd received a £250 Screwfix voucher for Crimbo. I said, whoa, whoa, whoa…before you get too excited, it's *not* a dating site.

We've just spent Christmas night binge-watching waste disposal commercials on YouTube. All we did was press Skip Ads…

With the Xmas party going downhill fast, I tried to spruce things up a bit by wrapping a packet of spaghetti in multiple sheets of paper. I said, right, who fancies a game of pasta parcel…?

The bloke who invented pass the parcel…you've got to hand it to him.

What's red and white and carries a machine-gun? Santa. I was lying about the machine-gun.

I've just seen a spectral presence, draped head to foot in season's greetings wrapping paper. Ooh look, I thought…the ghost of Christmas presents.

The missus bought me a copy of The Lion, the Witch for Crimbo. Apparently, there was a third off at the bookshop.

First white Christmas in decades and I nearly get knocked down by a snow plough. Watch where you're going, I shouted…through gritted teeth.

And the yuletide number one is…The Dandelion and Burdocks…live tonight…on Christmas Top of the *Pops*.

The wife gave me a megaphone for Crimbo. Whey hey, I thought…happy holler days!

I received sixteen Christmas presents in total and every one contained a faulty calculator. Hmmm, I thought…something doesn't add up.

My nephew's not happy I bought him an electrical sub-station for Crimbo. I wouldn't mind, like…but it was him who said he wanted a transformer.

A jar of black pepper just wished me happy Christmas. Talk about season's greetings…

My daughter got me a book called The Perils of Quicksand for Christmas. I can't wait to get stuck in.

Unsure what to watch Christmas Day night, I suggested a John McEnroe documentary. She said, *you cannot be serious*!

I love a bit of Peter Pan at Christmas…but it always gets me wondering what Captain Hook was called before he lost his hand?

The wife asked me to get her something containing diamonds for Crimbo. Unfortunately, I don't think a pack of playing cards was what she had in mind. The good news is the swelling is starting to go down now and the doctor says I might be out of hospital by the New Year…

I got er indoors an Egyptian Mummy covered in nuts, raisins and milk chocolate. You can't beat a bit of festive Pharaoh Rocher…

Cooking for twelve this Crimbo, I asked the wife what her favourite part was. She said, when it's all over.

I couldn't believe the missus spent £500 on a reincarnation correspondence course for me for Crimbo. Don't worry about it, she said…you only live once, don't you?

I woke up Christmas morning, thinking I was Coco the Clown. I reckon I must have slept funny…

We arrived twenty minutes early for our Christmas Day dinner date. Restaurant manager said, would you mind waiting a bit? I said, not at all. He said, marvellous…take this tray of drinks to table seven.

I got a model replica of Mount Kilimanjaro for Crimbo. Mate said, is it to scale? I said, no…just to look at.

Half way through cooking Christmas dinner, the missus jumped in the bath. Apparently she was doing what it said on the back of the sprouts packet…washing before use.

The girlfriend woke up Christmas morning with a huge smile on her face. Don't you just love permanent markers…?

I wasn't impressed with the golfing socks I got for Crimbo. There was a hole in one…

Christmas night and I accidentally took a swig of weedkiller instead of beer. The missus thought it was hilarious. Personally, I can't see the fungicide…

Honestly, there's no pleasing er indoors. She said she wanted a new wardrobe for Christmas, so I got her one from the second-hand shop…now she tells me it was blooming clothes she wanted.

Two cannibals, having an 80s pop star for Christmas dinner. One says, pity we've no bucks fizz. Other says, yeah…or Human League…or Duran Duran…or Shakin Stevens.

This Cockney was telling me how he'd been born within the sound of Baubles. I said, don't you mean Bow Bells? He said, no, I was born under a Christmas tree.

I rang my neighbour; I said, you couldn't pop out and give me a push, could you? He said, you do know it's Christmas morning, don't you? I said, I know that, but I *really* need your help. He said, alright then, where are you? I said, on my daughter's new swing at the bottom of the garden.

Christmas morning and the wife was going crazy, saying all her gold jewellery was missing. I said, don't look at me like that…it was you who told me to put some karats out for the reindeer.

My three-stone parrot died Christmas morning. Terrible news, like…but at least it's a weight off my shoulders.

What did I get for Crimbo? A cat o' flipping nine tails, that's what?. Ah well, there's only one thing for it. I'm off out on the lash…

I asked my daughter to pass the newspaper. She said, this is the twenty-first century. Try using the iPad I got for Crimbo instead. Five minutes later, she said, well, was it any good? I said, any good? That flipping fly never knew what hit it…

The mother-in-law walked in just as the big Christmas Day film was coming on. She said, Great Escape time, is it? About right, I thought;

ten minutes later, I was climbing out of the bedroom window and shimmying down the drainpipe en route to the boozer.

What's the difference between bogies and sprouts? Little boys won't eat sprouts.

I took my mate to A&E. I said, help, quick…he's choking on a Quality Street wrapper. Nurse said, purple one? I said, yup…that's him.

Alright, I'm obsessed with anagrams. So what? I just wanted to wish you a Ceramist's Myrrh…

I can't believe it. Christmas Day and the wife has left me on account of my constant paranoia. Oh, hang on a minute, she's back…she was just mixing us a snowball.

Christmas and work are two sides of the same coin. You do all the graft and some fat bloke in a suit gets all the credit.

Unsure what to get that tea leaf brother of mine for Crimbo, I just stuck an extra tenner in Nanny's purse for him.

We went in this restaurant and ordered Christmas dinner with all the trimmings. It came with balloons, tinsel, crepe paper and a side dish of baubles.

I bought the girlfriend a wooden leg for Christmas. It wasn't her main present…just a stocking-filler.

How bad is the TV at Christmas? Mine's just spent all day throwing up after a night at the pub.

We thought we'd give Zulu a blast Christmas Day night. Never again, I can tell you…it was all about a toilet attendant at Doncaster Wildlife Park.

Straight after, we watched The Exorcist and it scared me half to death. Now I'm worried what will happen if I put it on again.

The garage emailed me, saying my car was overdue a service. So I took it to midnight mass.

I dropped a stash of dodgy diamonds in my custard when the law came knocking Christmas Day. Bang to rights, the case went to court and I was found guilty as charged. The judge said the proof was in the pudding.

All I got for Crimbo was a bag of boiled sweets, so I went straight to the pub to drown my sorrows. Bar, humbug.

So I said, three-foot of snow and I had to work Christmas Day at the farm. It's a good job there was a slap-up dinner with all the trimmings to look forward to. He said, pigs in blankets, like? I said, no…but I made sure the sheepdog kept its coat on.

I bought the missus a fridge for Christmas. You should have seen her face light up when she opened it.

Christmas ghosts…they need to get a life.

What's red and white and invisible? No Santa!

Xmas dinner time and the wife only goes and serves up half portions. I said, what do you think you're doing, like? I said *gluten* free…not glutton!

Ooh argh! I wasn't impressed with the pirate DVD I purchased for Christmas night. There wasn't a pirate in sight…it was a blooming cowboy film!

I had the grandkids round Christmas Day, trying to get me to make a noise like a frog. Apparently their mum's told them that, when I croak it, they're off to Disneyland…

My new girlfriend invited me round for Christmas dinner. I said, homemade Yorkshire puddings? She said, Aunt Bessie's, actually. I said, is she the one who lives in the council flats on King's Road…?

I'm not saying Christmas Day queues in A&E were bad…but there was a bloke in front of me with a particularly nasty musket wound.

I was given a book for Christmas entitled: How To Finish Sentences with Beatles Lyrics. After reading it, I thought, well…that's two weeks of my life I won't Get Back.

Christmas Day and the wife leaves a note on the telly saying: it's not working, I'm leaving. I wouldn't mind, like…but I tried it and it came straight on.

I think the missus must have got the Christmas gift labels mixed up again. My five-year-old got a bottle of Jack Daniel's…while I finished up with a pair of Spiderman pyjamas.

Christmas Day and nothing on the telly as usual, I said, how about we open a couple of beers then stick some classic sci-fi on? She said, Intersteller? I said, I am, like…but I think I'd prefer a few glasses of home brew first.

I was having my customary Christmas Day argument with the mother-in-law when a wasp suddenly appeared, landing on her nose. I didn't let it sting her, like…I clobbered it first with the frying pan.

Unwrapping presents, I disturbingly discovered a severed head. The next present contained a torso. And the one after that an arm. And then a leg. Eyeing a big pile of unopened gifts, I thought, hmmm…something's definitely afoot.

We had Pancakes for Christmas dinner instead of turkey. It was alright, but I don't think the kids were too impressed…Pancakes was their favourite rabbit.

I went to get a beer from the fridge and thought I heard carrots and onions, singing Bee Gees songs. When I checked, it was just the chives talking…

This label on my new Christmas jim-jams said, 32 leg. I thought, crikey, that would fit four octopuses.

I've just seen Ebenezer Scrooge, running down the street with no clothes on. Talk about a mean streak…

Does anybody know anyone called Phillips? If so, can you please let him know I've been given his screwdriver set for Crimbo…?

Oh, and while you're at it, I've also got a coping saw, belonging to some other geezer called Stanley…

After I dropped an absolute beauty, the missus said, I wonder why turkey farts smell so bad? I said, it's for the hard of hearing, isn't it? I mean, they've got to have some way of knowing, haven't they…?

What yellow and highly dangerous and served with Christmas pudding? Shark infested custard.

I bought the missus some satin knickers for Christmas. She said, erm, if you think I'm wearing something pre-worn, you've another think coming…

Every Crimbo, we finish up with a ghost in the house. It must be the festive spirit.

Two cannibals, having Alan Sugar for Christmas dinner. One says, nice, innit? Other replies, nah…bit rich for me.

I can't believe I actually used to wake up Christmas morning and tell my parents I'd heard Santa. Honestly, they must have thought I was a right old numpty…

The missus got me a sofa bed for Crimbo. Well, she didn't really…I forgot to get her a present so she turned our existing sofa into a sofa bed.

Him: I swatted three flies Christmas morning: two males and a female. Her: How could you tell which was which? Him: The males were on a beer can and the female was on the phone.

I had the police round Christmas morning, complaining my dog was chasing a man on an electric scooter. I said, it can't be my dog…it hasn't even got an electric scooter.

The wife and I were discussing why Santa is always portrayed as a man. I said, it's obvious, isn't it? I mean, would a woman wear the same clothes every Christmas…?

After a terrible Xmas dinner out, we were left waiting nearly an hour for our sweet. So I said to this waiter, can you tell me how long our chocolate logs will be? He said, I don't know…I've not measured them.

Last night's fancy dress party was a blast. I went as Tin Man from Wizard of Oz and finished up well oiled…

I've just seen two festive bell ringers, having a fight. Honestly, they were having a right old ding-dong.

Spud and a sprout on the boil. Sprout says, warm in here, innit? Spud says, I didn't know sprouts could talk.

I was explaining to my daughter how it's better to give than receive. She said, yeah, well…I don't think it is.

That jigsaw puzzle I got for Christmas. 6-8 years it said on the box…I had it done in two hours.

I wasn't impressed with Trading Places. It was all about a flatfish salesman on Grimsby docks.

Russian nativity dolls…they're so full of themselves.

Couple walking down the street in barcode fancy dress. I said, excuse me…are you two an item?

Two relaxing days off for Crimbo but it's back to the bakery in the morning. Yup, it's a wonderful loaf…

3 o'clock Boxing Day morning and I had the next-door neighbour round, banging the door down. It's a good job I was still up…practising on my new bagpipes.

I was punched on the nose by a bloke in Tyson Fury costume. I thought, it's never Boxing Day already, is it…?

Unbelievable. Still 364 days to Christmas and some saddos have already got their lights up.

Bloke at the bar, walloping double whisky and coke. I said, you wouldn't be drinking like that if you'd got what I've got. He said, what's that? I said, forty-eight pence…

The booze wasn't half flying at the Argentinian footballer themed Boxing Day party. I thought, this could definitely get Messi…

I asked a bloke in a dragon costume what his favourite Christmas band was. Put it this way, he said…it's definitely not slayed.

Two crows, eyeing a snowman. One says, are you sure it's not a human? Other replies, course I am…it's not on its phone.

Police have confirmed the man who tragically fell from an open window on the 18th floor of a Boxing Day nightclub definitely wasn't a bouncer…

I was telling my mate how I got absolutely hammered, watching classic sitcoms on the telly. He said, Last of the Summer Wine? I said, actually, it was a bottle of vodka the gaffer got me for Crimbo.

With massive queues at the bar, I went to the fancy dress shop next door and rented a tennis ball costume. I got served straight away…

I said to the missus, get your coat on…it's Christmas and it's time for the pub. She said, do you mean you're taking me? I said, no…I'm turning the blooming heating off.

Two piles of vomit outside a boozer. One says, we're lost, aren't we? Other replies, are we heckers like…I was brought up round here.

So I said, I must have had a few Boxing Day, because I was well ripped off by that new Irish barman. He said, oh, really? I said, it was O'Reilly, actually…and just you wait till I catch up with him.

Newsflash: Xmas getaway revellers have made off with £1000 worth of in-flight drinks from Leeds-Bradford Airport. Spanish police have been warned to keep a look-out for anyone concealing a can of diet coke, a quarter bottle of whisky and two small tins of lager.

A bloke in hippopotamus fancy dress goes in a pub and orders a pint of beer. Landlord says, a talking hippo, eh? We don't get many of your type in here. Hippopotamus replies, I'm not surprised with these prices!

Bloke in a tiger costume comes in next and says, I'll have…a pint of lager, please. Landlord says, why the big pause? Tiger throws its legs in the air and says, don't ask me…I was born with them!

Bloke in Quasi Modo fancy dress orders a double whiskey. Barman says, Glenfiddich? He says, the Bells! The Bells!

I was telling my mate how the other half lost the gold necklace I bought her for Crimbo. He said, choker, like? I said, choke her? Hardly…but I blooming felt like it, I can tell you.

I'm not saying I had too much to drink Boxing Day…but when I got up next morning, I needed sunglasses on to open the fridge.

Out in highwayman fancy dress, I challenged a bloke in a Bart Simpson costume to a duel. When he ran off, I shouted after him: what are you…*yellow*?

I rang the wife; I said, that new T-shirt I got for Crimbo. I've spilled ketchup down the front and need to get it in the wash. What setting shall I use? She said, what's it say on it? I said, Oasis, Reunion Tour, 2025…

The doctor warned me to watch my drinking over Christmas. So I did. I found a boozer with a great big mirror in it.

I went to a fancy dress party as a loaf of bread. The birds were all over me…

Liver: you need to stop drinking. Me: And you need to calm the **** down!

Two wallahs in RAF costumes, having a scrap outside a boozer. Ooh look, I thought…fighter pilots.

I gave this waiter a piece of broken snooker cue. I said, before you say anything…you wanted a tip, didn't you?

Did you know that nine out of ten people confess to drinking too much alcohol at Christmas? Staggering.

I went to buy a new car in the Boxing Day sales. Salesman said, good choice. Now…shall we talk turkey?

Driving home, I spotted this sign saying: Mud on Road. I turned the corner and there was this 70s glam rock band, singing Lonely This Christmas.

I went to the boozer and asked if they did cash back. I said, because if you do, can I have the hundred nicker I spent Christmas Eve? The blooming wife won't shut up about it…

Sick to the back teeth of turkey, I paid a visit to Burger King. I said, give us a couple of whoppers, pal. Assistant said, if you insist, sir…you're a handsome devil and I can tell just by looking at you that you're a big hit with the ladies.

Bloke at the bar with a toilet strapped to his back, buying everybody Christmas drinks. He was obviously feeling a bit flush…

Message for whoever nicked my shoes while I was having a go on the Wacky Warehouse Boxing Day bouncy castle…just grow up, can't you?

I was trying on the new shoes I got for Crimbo. I said, they still feel a bit tight to be fair. She said, try them with the tongue out. I said, I'm athraid th'till a bit on th'tight tide…

Warning: if you receive an email from me, offering free Boxing Day tickets to watch Sheffield Wednesday, don't open it. It contains free Boxing Day tickets to watch Sheffield Wednesday.

Stopped by the police, I was asked to do a random breath test. I said, if it's random, pal…how come you don't ask one of the passengers?

Did you hear about the footballer with two left feet? His wife bought him a pair of flip-flips for Christmas.

When I came down with a terrible bout of Christmas man flu, the missus insisted upon rubbing my chest with Vic. It helped, like…but I came out in awful rash from his stubbly chin.

Boxing Day morning and I bumped into Elvis in B&Q. He was returning a sander.

Alright, so I bought two hundred helium-filled balloons for the Xmas party. I admit it…I got carried away a bit.

I bumped into my doctor in the pub. He said, you do know you've got a severe iron deficiency, don't you? I said, how can you tell that from just looking at me? He said, because your clothes are all creased…

Off to the Boxing Day sales, I passed 23 signs in a row, all saying: Reduce Speed Now. Well, it must have worked, because when I went in HMV, I spotted the Keanu Reeves film of the same title in the bargain bucket, priced just £1.99.

I must have had a few last night. I won the disco dancing competition and I was only going to the bar…

I'm not saying I've banged weight on…but the wife is using the Wok she got for Christmas to iron my shirts in.

The missus got me some PC World vouchers for Christmas. Blimey, you've got to be careful what you say in that place, haven't you…?

Does anyone know if Hugh ever showed up at Mariah Carey's? I sincerely hope so…it sounds like it's all she wanted for Christmas.

I phoned the quacks; I said, that haemorrhoid cream you prescribed caused a really bad reaction. He said, where did you apply it? I said, on the front row during the interval of Dick Whittington.

Spending the festive season in Amsterdam, I booked a table for dinner; I said to the girlfriend, seeing as we're in Holland, shall we go Dutch? She said, *niet in een miljoen jaar; je kan betalen.*

She said, do you know you left the Christmas tree lights on again last night, dearest? I said, sorry, darling, it's just that, well…I'm having trouble switching off at night.

If you're looking for a decent festive read, I can heartily recommend Christmas Movie Classics by…yup, you've got it, Homer Lone.

Anyone got a mop and bucket? That Sports Direct mug I got for Crimbo…I've just knocked it over and flooded the house out.

So I said, I'm off on a right do New Year's Eve: a fiver in and drink as much as you want. He said, where's that, like? I said, the local swimming baths.

I was given a boxset of American drama series Lost for Christmas. Now I can't find it…

Right, that's it. No more chocolate for me this Christmas…it makes my clothes shrink.

I fell down drunk Christmas Eve and broke my arm in two places…once in the pub and then again in the takeaway.

My best pal died over Crimbo after overdosing on heartburn remedies. I can't believe it…Gav is gone!

This bloke asked me what I did for a living. I said, I'm a Hogmanay sky rocket designer. He said, straight up, like? I said, what do you think...?

After spending the majority of the festive season as the rear end of a pantomime horse, I've decided to quit...while I'm a head.

When I worked in pantomime, I became addicted to trap doors. Thankfully it was just a stage I was going through.

I went to the newsagents and asked if they had the latest edition of Pantomime Monthly. Assistant said, it's behind you...

I've booked me and the girlfriend a table for New Year's Day. Let's hope she likes snooker.

That new telly we bought for Crimbo has packed in already. Built in Antenna, it said on the box. It's the last time I'll be buying any of that foreign muck, I can tell you...

I'm proud to say I'm officially in the Guinness Book of Records. Yup, I drunk more of the black stuff over Crimbo than anyone else in the country.

Last night's Christmas party: I had a go at that snorting coke lark, but called it a day when the bubbles kept going up my nose...

The amazing Christmas night drama about foul play in a tomato sauce factory; if anyone missed it, it's still available on Ketchup TV.

So I said, I'm off on a duck do New Year's Eve. He said, what's a duck do, like? I said, quack-quack, quack-quack...

A lorry load of porcelain pigeons was involved in a collision with a lorry load of ceramic doves. Both vehicles are a turtle right off...

I don't think the wife quite got it when I asked her to turn the Christmas lights on. Next thing, she was dressed in her best pink negligée, dancing seductively under the tree.

I pulled a tuft of nostril hair to see if it hurt. Judging by the reaction of the woman sitting next to me at Jack and the Beanstalk…I'd say it probably did.

Walking home from the boozer with my mate, I spotted a gang of youths following us. I said, I reckon we're going to get mugged here. He said, I think you might be right…oh, and before I forget, here's that twenty quid I borrowed Christmas Eve.

I bet the missus £100 I'd have a Christmas number one. She lost. Three tins of air freshener it took her to shift the stench in the bathroom…

This security guard stopped me on the way out of Morrisons. He said, you've just nicked a Christmas cake, haven't you? I said, you mean Stollen? He said, dress it up how you want, pal…but you're not leaving here without paying for it.

Apparently the Grinch grows his own vegetables. I can't say I'm surprised. He's always been green fingered.

Speaking of which, ET's been caught shoplifting over Crimbo. Again, no surprise. I always said he was light-fingered…

That prescription the quack gave me to cure my Christmas constipation; an hour later I was on the blower to the suppository helpline. Seriously, how rude were they? They told me to shove them up my ***e!

My grandad was telling me how he got an apple and orange for Crimbo. I thought, who could *possibly* want the latest iPhone on a defunct network…?

Apparently there's a nudist convention in town between Christmas and New Year. I might pop down if I've nothing on.

The wife went nuts when I swapped her Celebrations sweet wrappers round for a laugh. Honestly, she didn't half get her Snickers in a Twix…

I'm in the bad books with er indoors again. After a crap Crimbo, I promised I'd make it up to her by taking her into town to look for

some cheap flights. Honestly, you should have seen her face when we walked in the darts shop…

This bloke asked me which I preferred: warm cider or warm wine? I said, I take it this is a mull-tipple choice question…?

Apparently a policeman is assaulted in town fifteen or twenty times every Christmas. If I was him, I think I'd be looking for another job…

DasherDancerPrancerVixenCometCupidDonnerBlitzenRudolphJerusalem is my new computer password. Apparently it had to be nine characters long and include one capital.

The wife left me after I spent Christmas vegged out in front of the telly, watching Hollywood boxing films. She's back now, like…we were just going through a Rocky patch.

My little brother, Sid, lost his ID over Christmas. Now we just call him S…

Hand-painted Muhammad Ali figurine for sale. £50. Unwanted Christmas present. Not boxed.

I'm not saying the wife's put a fortune on her credit card over Crimbo…but she's caused a run on the pound.

Newsflash: The bloke who invented the TV remote control died just before Christmas. He was found two weeks later down the back of the settee…

I bought the missus a pampering session for Crimbo. Big mistake. As soon as she walked into the hotel, everybody started pelting her with disposable nappies…

I'm not saying I've slapped weight on over Christmas…but I've just been stopped on my way out of the bowling alley and been accused of having a ball up my top.

He said, twenty years ago, the other half gave me this wonderful garment for Christmas and it still fits perfectly today. I said, mate…it's a flipping scarf.

I went online, looking for hangover remedies. Take two tablets with a glass of water was the top answer. Now I'm in A&E, waiting for a couple of iPads to be surgically removed…

The wife left me after I ate her Quality Streets. I reckon this calls for a Celebration…

Every festive season our house is haunted by a spectral presence, carrying a bunch of red, purple and white flowers. It must be the ghost of Christmas fuchsia…

A pal of mine asked what I got up to over Crimbo. I said, I spent most nights on the tiles. He said, but I thought you were teetotal? I said, I am…but I'm also a cat burglar.

Bob Geldof goes to the chemist for a box of plasters. Assistant says, Band Aid? He says, yup, charity supergroup and one of the biggest selling Christmas songs ever. Now…these plasters.

I went to the travel agents. I said, I want to stop at the hotel where Kevin McCallister stayed in Home Alone Two. Assistant said, Big Apple? I said, no, thanks…I've just had my dinner.

I dropped a £20 note my nan gave me for Crimbo and chased it for half an hour in gale force winds. I didn't catch it, like…but at least I had a good run for my money.

Question 7 in the Crimbo pub quiz was: name the perpetrators of the Great Train Robbery. I knew the answer, like, but decided to pass…I'm not a grass.

That Australian beer night at the pub; I wasn't keen on the kangaroo branded lager…all I could taste was hops.

I had a gas service engineer round over Christmas. I said, are you fully licensed? He said, absolutely, sir. I said, marvellous…I'll have a pint of lager and whisky chaser, please.

Black bull goes into a boozer. Barman says, we nearly named our pub after you, mate. Black Bull says, what, Ralph…?

Er, whoever stole the mirror from the gent's toilet needs to take a long, hard look at themselves…

I was invited to a cannibal themed fancy dress party. We started off with a finger buffet.

Newsflash: Police were called to break up a New Year's Eve party attended by hundreds of people in sick bird of prey costumes. A spokesman has confirmed it was an ill eagle rave…

Staggering home blind drunk at 3 o'clock New Year's Day morning, I was greeted by the missus, who said she'd missed me. Normally that would be a good thing. Then I saw her reloading…

I can't believe it's New Year's Day tomorrow. It's taken me until now to get used to the current one…

This bloke was telling me how he self-identified as an iPhone, then went out to celebrate the New Year and managed to get himself arrested. I said, were you charged? He said, was I heckers like…I was only on seven per cent battery.

With blizzard conditions forecast for the New Year, please, please, please don't forget the old Eskimo saying…don't drink yellow snow.

I asked this bloke at the bar if he'd done his chores. He said, chores? What chores? I said, that's very nice of you, pal…I'll have a double rum and coke, please.

I went on Hogmanay caveman-themed fancy dress stag do. We went clubbing…

Two blokes in Mexican bandolero costumes, waiting at a bus stop in the pouring rain. Ooh look, I thought…it's the Wet Bandits.

All this talk about plastic banknotes lasting longer than paper ones is utter nonsense. Two pints and whisky chasers later and that was twenty gone the same as usual…

I walked in a boozer with a pint of beer on my head and a G&T on each shoulder. I said, the drinks are on me…

Bloke in Pope fancy dress accosted by a youth, asking if he can help with his hearing. Pope places hands over the youth's ears, says a prayer, then says, how's your hearing now? Youth says, I don't know…it's not till next Friday.

Last night's statue themed fancy dress party…seriously, you couldn't move.

New Year's Eve and I received a text, saying the girlfriend was in Casualty. So I rushed home, stuck the telly on and didn't move for an hour. There were plenty of doctors and nurses about, like…but no sign of the girlfriend. So I got my coat back on and went straight to the pub.

I went out New Year's Eve in tarantula fancy dress. Don't bother asking what time I crawled in.

After piling weight on over Christmas, it didn't half cheer me up to read that 60% of the human body is water. It means I'm not fat, after all…I'm just flooded.

We had the Beach Boys in the boozer over Crimbo. Even better, they were buying everybody drinks. All you could hear was, round-round get a round, I get a round, yeah, get a round-round-round, I get a round…

I booked a Hogmanay table for two at a Michelin style restaurant. I said, we'll both have a medium-well cross-ply with all the trimmings, please…

I went to a kickboxer's New Year's Eve party. It was a right old knees-up…

23rd February and I've only just had my Christmas dinner. That's the last time you'll catch me using a slow cooker, I can tell you.

My New Year's resolution is to read more and I'm pleased to announce I've already made a start. Yup, I've put subtitles on the telly.

I'm not saying the missus and I were at each other's throats over Christmas…but we've just had UN Peacekeepers move in next door.

After an argument strewn Christmas, I was starting to think the wife had developed Tourette's. Now I've found out she really *does* want me to ** off!**

I went out New Year's Eve in a screwdriver costume. I didn't half turn a few heads.

The wife suggested putting the latest Marvel movie on New year's Day night. I said, I never knew there were any films about powdered milk…

Last night's NYE party: there was one bloke dressed as a chicken and another dressed as an egg, having a race round the block. I thought, hmmm…now this *is* going to be interesting.

I keep driving my car into walls, making sure the cost of repairs outstrips my income, meaning I haven't any money left for food. Yup, I'm on a New Year crash diet.

That hokey-cokey alarm clock I got for Crimbo. It's alright, like…but it takes me two hours to get out of bed.

After spending our first Xmas together, the missus has come to the conclusion I've got two big faults. Number one I don't listen, plus some other crap she was going on about…

The bad news is I've been diagnosed with a flesh-eating bug. The good news is I've put so much weight on over Xmas I've been given forty-eight years to live.

I told the missus my fitness instructor had recommended I start walking ten miles per day in order to shift the Xmas blubber. Great news, she said…that means this time next week you'll be seventy miles away.

With Crimbo done, I enrolled at the gym and was told to wear loose-fitting clothing. I said, if I had any loose-fitting clothing, pal, I wouldn't be here now, would I…?

My nutritionist says I should only eat 1200 calories per day. I said, no problem…what about at night?

I spent my entire Christmas, hunting down a spider in the kitchen. It wasn't until the New Year that I realised my glasses were cracked.

After all the eating and drinking I did over Crimbo…I'm happy to report that my socks still fit.

First day back at work after Christmas, I always feel a bit flat. This year more than ever…after being run over by a steamroller.

I couldn't wait when the missus booked us a holiday to celebrate the New Year. Unfortunately, due to an unfortunate spacing error at the travel agents, we've just spent two weeks on Norfolk B roads…

After a rotten Christmas, I told my policewoman girlfriend the spark had gone out of our relationship. So she tasered me…

I banged so much weight on at Christmas, I made an urgent appointment with a nutritionist. She said, don't eat anything fatty. I said, what, burgers, chips and stuff? She said, no, don't eat anything…Fatty!

Me: Alexa, remind me to enrol at the gym. Alexa: I have added gin to your shopping list. Me: that's near enough…

I decided to enrol with weightwatchers online. Question one was: do you accept cookies? I replied: is this a trick question…?

I didn't reckon much to that yo-yo dieting lark. Every time I swallowed one, it came straight back up again.

New Year's Day and there's a sign up at the gym saying: closed due to short staff. I thought, why can't they just employ a few taller people?

I can't say I recommend Christmas dinner by candlelight. It took three months to cook the turkey.

I've just been banned from water aerobics classes for peeing in the pool. The lifeguard shouted so loud I nearly fell in.

So I said, this flipping egg diet isn't going too well. She said, free range, like? I said, no…Cadbury's.

I've just burned a thousand calories in half an hour. Silly me…I forgot to take the pizza out of the oven.

I went to the doctors after pouring fabric conditioner over my Christmas dinner, Boxing Day tea and New Year's Eve buffet. Quack said, hmmm…sounds like a chronic case of Comfort eating to me.

If anyone is seeking post-Christmas keep-fit inspiration, try taking a leaf out of my Nan's book, who's been walking twenty miles per day since I was five years old. Last I heard, she was somewhere on the outskirts of Buenos Aires…

Twelve days of Christmas and I managed a Marathon every day…or Snickers as they're known nowadays.

I always commence gym sessions with fifteen minutes of stretching, pulling and bending. After I've got my kit on, I usually have half an hour rest then make a start…

New Year fitness tip: stick your fit-bit in the tumble dryer every morning. An average cycle is over 5000 steps.

Other than that, you could always volunteer for bin day retrieval duties, burning excess calories by dragging said wheelie from the next flipping postcode!

I made a New Year's resolution to drink more water. So far I've only got as far as the drink more bit…

Enrolling at the gym was the best thing I ever did and I'm loving the new machine they've got. It's full of fizzy pop, crisps and every chocolate bar imaginable.

I've just started an Adam Ant New Year diet. You can eat what you want but…don't chew ever, don't chew ever…

After slamming weight on over Crimbo, I made a beeline for the doctors. He said, it looks like you've got an over active, erm, erm…I said, thyroid gland? He said, no…knife and fork!

My new year fitness regime is finally up and running. Two hours I spent on the treadmill this morning. My goal for tomorrow is to actually turn it on…

I went to the travel agents, looking for advice about booking a trip to the States. Assistant said, New Jersey is amazing. I said, that's nice of you to say…the wife got it me for Christmas.

I never thought I was the type to get up at six and go for a beat the flab five-mile run. I was right…I wasn't.

Right, that's it. Dry January it is. Thirty-one days to go until my next bath…

So I said, he's got the sack. He said, who? I said, Father Christmas…

Ah, good old Father Christmas…he's definitely got a gift.